A Canadian Heraldic Primer

Kevin Greaves

Illustrated by
Bruce Patterson and Gordon Macpherson

Published by the
Heraldry Society of Canada

Additional copies of this book can be purchased from:
The Heraldry Society of Canada
P.O. Box 2128, Station T
Ottawa, Ontario, Canada K1G 3H9

Logos of the Toronto Maple Leaf and Montréal Canadiens Hockey organizations are used with their kind permission.

Layout and typography by MacNamara Design, Toronto.
Printed in Canada.

Canadian Cataloguing in Publication Data

Greaves, Kevin, 1931-
A Canadian heraldic primer

Includes bibliographic references.
ISBN 0-9693063-4-2

1. Heraldry. 2. Heraldry—Canada.
I. Heraldry Society of Canada. II. Title.

CR212.G75 2000   929.6   C00-900137-9

Message from the Governor General

As one who has had the pleasure of designing a personal coat of arms, I now understand more clearly some of the concepts that lie behind the magic of this ancient form of art and identity.

The possibility that we can, through heraldry, represent the ideas closest to our heart and salute important parts of our heritage in an imperishable form, is a powerful and attractive one. More and more Canadians are taking up this idea, as witnessed by the number of requests for new coats of arms received from individuals and institutions each year.

Beyond these are the many thousands who want to know more about heraldry. How did it originate, how is it structured, how is it unfolding and evolving in Canada now that we have our own state authority?

I want to congratulate author Kevin Greaves and the artists, Bruce Patterson and Gordon Macpherson for producing such a lively and amusing introduction to the topic and for including so much material on Canadian heraldry. I am pleased to have my own arms included among the illustrations.

At the same time, I want to congratulate the Heraldry Society of Canada for this important educational initiative. Since 1966, it has played a key role in ensuring that Canadians have access to current information on heraldry and encouraging its proper acquisition, use and display.

With all good wishes for future endeavours.

Adrienne Clarkson

Adrienne Clarkson
Governor General of Canada

Sponsors

The Heraldry Society would like to express its deepest
appreciation to the following foundations and individuals
who have sponsored the publication of this book
through their generous donations.

FOUNDATION SPONSORS

The W. Garfield Weston Foundation

The Jackman Foundation

The Sovereign Order of St. John of Jerusalem,
Knights Hospitaller, Priory of Eastern Canada

INDIVIDUAL SPONSORS

Ralph Brocklebank   Jean Matheson
Robert Gibson   John Udd
Peter Liddle   Ben Weider
Roger A. Lindsay   John Wilkes
          Cyril Woods

AN ADDITIONAL THANK-YOU

In addition to the sponsors listed above, the Society is
most grateful to more than eighty other members
who have helped to make the *Primer* a reality through their
generous contributions to our education program.

Foreword by the Chief Herald of Canada

There is a small but influential stream linking heraldry and humour in English language heraldic studies since World War II. The leading example of the genre is Moncreiffe and Pottinger's *Simple Heraldry*, a wonderful introduction to the art and science which continues to inform and delight readers in the tens of thousands.

Kevin Greaves, Bruce Patterson and Gordon Macpherson have, to a considerable degree, been inspired by this example with, I think you will agree, fine results. They not only cover known territory in a lively way, but introduce new material in an accessible and very effective manner

But this primer is significant at a deeper level because its essential aim is to reach out to a wider public and to interest those who have heard of heraldry but have only a minimal understanding of it. This worthy objective directly reflects the ongoing mission of the Heraldry Society of Canada to introduce as many Canadians as possible to the magic of heraldry with the ultimate aim of imbedding heraldry more deeply in the Canadian experience. For this reason alone, I am eager to offer congratulations not only to the author and artists but to the Society for the publication of this work.

Those with more knowledge of heraldry, who will also undoubtedly read this, will find much that is familiar, although expressed in a lively and engaging way; but there is important new information too. This is the first book with extensive references to the evolving story of Canadian heraldry. My colleagues and I hope it will be the first of many.

Robert D. Watt
Chief Herald of Canada
The Chancellery
Ottawa, 2000

Preface

This primer is aimed at students and others who may have heard a little about heraldry and are curious about it, but are put off by the seriousness, academic tone and sheer size of the standard heraldic texts—and perhaps by the hushed reverence with which the subject is sometimes discussed by its proponents. Heraldry is a fascinating hobby which is also a great deal of fun and there is no need to take it too seriously. However, like any other hobby, you need to know some facts and background in order to get the most out of it. This book is intended to give a short, slightly irreverent account of heraldry, with the hope of giving at least a flavour of this intriguing subject and perhaps whetting a few appetites.

The primer is published under the auspices of the Heraldry Society of Canada. Membership in the Society is available – and invaluable – to anyone who finds himself (or herself) hooked, as I am, by this ancient art form.

K.W.G.
Hamilton, 2000

ACKNOWLEDGEMENT
The author and illustrators would be less than gracious if they failed to acknowledge their debt to Iain Moncreiffe and Don Pottinger, the creators of that superb introduction to heraldry, *Simple Heraldry, Cheerfully Illustrated*. They were the first to introduce the saving gift of humour to a subject too often associated with dryness and pedantry. Theirs is deservedly the first book noted in the bibliography.

Contents

Chapter 1: How heraldry got started

Many people know that the ancient art of heraldry involves designs painted on a shield and used to identify the owner, but how did it start? The shield itself is the oldest form of personal defence and soldiers from time immemorial have decorated their shields in various ways. We know, for instance, that the ancient Greeks painted things on their shields; so was this a form of heraldry? No, not really, because, while such a design might identify the owner of the shield, there was nothing to prevent two people from having identical shields—unless of course, one defeated the other in combat. Moreover, the shield paintings of this early period were not in general passed on from father to son (i.e. hereditary), thereby lacking one of the key features of true heraldry. Heraldry as we understand it really did not develop until some time in the early 1100s, at a time when knights started using closed helmets that completely hid their faces, much as hockey goalies do today.

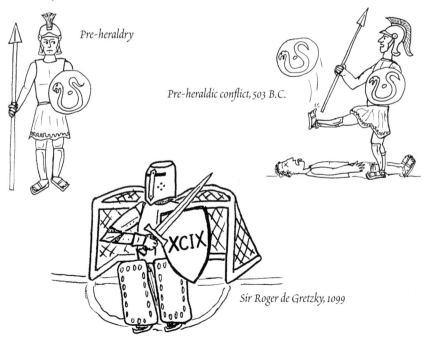

Pre-heraldry

Pre-heraldic conflict, 503 B.C.

Sir Roger de Gretzky, 1099

Pre-heraldic spectator confusion

THE TOURNAMENT

While the requirements of warfare may have contributed to the process, it was the popularity of the TOURNAMENT that, more than anything else, led to the birth of heraldry. These colourful mock-warfare contests, with all their pomp and panoply, were the great spectator sport of the late Middle Ages—the mediaeval equivalent of hockey or football. Sponsored by the king or one of the great nobles, tournaments featured knights clobbering one another in groups (the mêlée) or singly (the joust). The only problem was that one knight in armour looked much like any other, so that the spectators couldn't tell the good guys from the bad guys. As a result, knights started painting things on their shields to identify themselves, and these devices* tended to become permanently associated with the individual knight—in much the same way that his lucky number may become attached to a star athlete today. Not infrequently, a son might wish to use the device that his father had made famous in the joust or in war. However this was a bit hit-and-miss at first (depending largely as it did on the athletic prowess of dear old dad) so the hereditary feature required a further boost to become a fixed part of heraldry.

THE SEAL

That boost was the SEAL or SIGNET used on legal documents. At a time when almost everybody was illiterate and when even the great nobles could rarely sign their names, it became customary for a

---

* DEVICE and CHARGE are fancy heraldic terms with essentially the same meaning: *"thing, when used as a part of a heraldic design."*

The Seal in use

The Seal in transmission

Heraldic conflict, 1390

man to put the distinctive device of his shield on the seal that he used for his civil transactions. It became, in effect, his signature. Since most legal documents of the period concerned land—which was inherited under rigid rules—it became a matter of practical convenience for a son, on inheriting his father's lands, to continue to use the particular shield-device that had become associated with the ownership of those lands. In this way, a man's ARMS (the shield with its distinctive design) became recognized as part of his personal property and therefore inheritable like any other property. However, there was as yet no system to prevent two knights, possibly from different parts of the country, from selecting identical devices for their arms. Such a system did develop quite quickly, however, and involved certain gentlemen called HERALDS.

The Herald as sportscaster

The Herald as bureaucrat

THE HERALDS

Since the king or noble sponsoring a tournament was much too grand to organize and run it himself, he would appoint one of his retainers to do it for him. This officer was known as a HERALD (i.e. announcer or proclaimer) since one of his jobs was to announce the names of the contestants before each bout and to proclaim the winner when it was over, much as a radio or T.V. sportscaster does today. Since the herald could not see the faces of the helmeted knights, he had to rely on the devices on their shields to recognize them. For this reason, he had to familiarize himself with the shield-devices of any knights who might conceivably show up at his tournaments and, eventually, to become *the* knowledgeable expert in the field—a field that was soon to be named HERALDRY.

As more and more knights and nobles began to use arms (some now only for personal identification, quite apart from the tournament), it was natural that they would go to the heralds for advice. This was partly to ensure that their new design was not the same as one already used by another knight, but also to be sure that it was "correct" (note that bureaucracy was already becoming a power in the Middle Ages). So now the heralds were becoming involved, not only with the recognition of arms, but with their design as well.

Eventually however, this form of control by individual heralds proved inadequate and the duplication of arms and consequent disputes—sometimes violent—began to occur. To prevent this, monarchs began to declare that arms could only be granted with royal assent and appointed senior heralds, known as KINGS OF ARMS, to look after it for them.

USE ON ACCOUTREMENTS

As heraldry became more and more popular, the shield-design was frequently used on other parts of a knight's accoutrements, as for example on the cloth surcoat that he wore over his armour (which accounts for the term COAT OF ARMS). It was also used on the trappings of his horse, on his personal flag or banner and even in the dress of his wife.

Surcoat   *Horse*   *Wife*

HERALDIC ACHIEVEMENT

Crest

Wreath or Torse

Helm or Helmet

Dexter Supporter

Shield or Arms

Mantling

Sinister Supporter

Compartment

Motto Scroll

MOTTO

This illustration shows how the elements of a heraldic "achievement" go together. Refer to it while reading Chapter 2. Note that "dexter" (right) and "sinister" (left) are considered from the point of view of the bearer of the shield, not that of the observer.

Chapter 2: The heraldic achievement

S o far we have only talked about the shield and its devices, but other elements gradually became added to the shield to form what is known as the ACHIEVEMENT OF ARMS.

THE CREST

The term "crest" is often misused to refer to the whole heraldic achievement of an individual. In fact, it is only part of it, the bit on the top. The crest developed originally from a fan-shaped metal plate that some knights attached to their helmets to deflect a sword-blow to the head. At first, these were quite plain, but soon people started painting animals or birds on them and cutting the plates to the outline of the device. These flat plates could only be seen properly in profile, however, so it was only a simple step to fashioning the device "in the round" from wood or boiled leather and attaching it to the helmet with rivets. So was born the heraldic CREST which, when used in tournaments, soon became another identifying feature of the jousting knight. In the painted records kept by the heralds, the crest soon became a regular feature, being depicted above the shield, the position it occupies today. While each individual still required a distinctive shield, it became quite a common practice for the members of a particular family to use the same crest, so the frequently misused term "family crest" *may* be quite correct, so long as it refers only to the device that goes *above* the shield, not to the shield itself.

The evolution of the crest

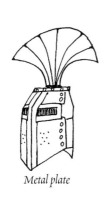

Metal plate

Moulded crest

Crest as part of a coat of arms

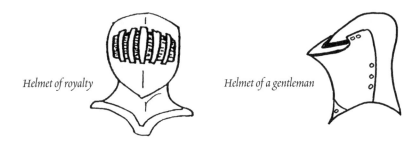

Helmet of royalty

Helmet of a gentleman

THE HELMET, MANTLE AND WREATH

As heraldry evolved from being used only in tournaments and battle, people began painting their arms on all sorts of objects and the heralds started recording them on parchment "rolls of arms". At first, there would be just the shield, then the shield and crest, and then the artists started showing the crest attached to its helmet. Early on, the choice of the helmet was up to the artist and in most cases showed the style of helmet popular at the time. Later, it became a custom that the type of helmet would indicate the rank of the bearer—as a member of royalty, a peer, a knight, or a gentleman. Of these, only two are likely to be seen in Canada: the gold, full-faced, barred helmet that denotes sovereignty on our Canadian coat of arms, and the steel, side-facing closed helmet that denotes the individual—the usual helmet granted by the Canadian Heraldic Authority. Along with the helmet, there is usually shown what is known as the MANTLE or MANTLING. This originated as a piece of cloth that was often attached to the helmet below the crest and hung down over the shoulders to keep the heat of the sun off the armour. This was held in place by a WREATH of twisted silk which

A hot knight

Realistic mantling

Tattered mantling

also hid the unsightly join between crest and helmet. In depictions of arms, both mantle and wreath are traditionally shown in the two main colours of the arms, with the mantling rather tattered as if hacked about in battle. In fact, most heraldic artists nowadays show the mantling in a highly stylized fashion, so "tattered" that its original form has almost disappeared and it appears as a sort of ribbon-like decoration.

SUPPORTERS AND COMPARTMENT

For the first three centuries of heraldry, the shield and crest, with its associated helmet, wreath and mantling, formed the whole of the heraldic achievement. Then, about the middle of the 15th century, certain nobles began to display another element of their arms, known as SUPPORTERS. These were usually in the form of animal or human figures standing on either side of the shield and, so to speak, "supporting" it. Originally, the supporters were just placed on either side of the shield with nothing to support *them*, but later they were provided with a grassy knoll to stand on and this became known as the COMPARTMENT. The latter quite soon became the resting place for symbolic devices for which room could not be found in the balance of the achievement—such as the mayflowers and thistles in the arms of Nova Scotia and wild roses in those of Alberta. In England, personal supporters are largely restricted to the peerage and certain knightly orders. Canada, with neither peers nor knights, restricts them to eminent persons such as Governors General, Lieutenant Governors, Privy Councillors and the like, plus the senior ranks of the Orders of Canada and Military Merit; and these are for life only and cannot be inherited. However, many corporate bodies such as commercial corporations, universities, pro-

Unsupported supporters

Supported supporters, with compartment
(Province of Nova Scotia)

fessional associations and municipalities are also entitled to a grant of supporters.

THE MOTTO

Most coats of arms display some sort of motto, often—but by no means always—in Latin. Most are brief phrases expressing some pious, loyal or moral sentiment, or may play on the name of the bearer or on the main device of the shield or crest. Mottoes are usually displayed on scrolls either below the shield (the English tradition) or above it (the Scottish tradition), at the pleasure of the individual. There may even be two mottoes, one above and one below. Mottoes, while part of a grant of arms in Scotland and Canada, are not considered of major importance and it is quite possible for two persons of quite different families to have the same motto.

English motto location

Scottish motto location

THE HERALDIC ACHIEVEMENT

To sum up, a complete coat of arms or heraldic *Achievement* may consist of some eight parts: the *shield*; the *helmet, mantling* and *wreath*; the *crest;* the *supporters* and *compartment;* and the *motto.* (See the illustration on page 6.) Not all, or even most, achievements are this complex, however. Most Canadian personal arms do not have supporters and without supporters there is no need for a compartment. It is quite possible, indeed, for an achievement to consist of nothing but the shield and this is common in arms originating in France, where the crest was little used. If there is a crest, it is not obligatory to display it with a helmet and mantling, although it is always shown arising from a wreath. A grant of arms will customarily show every element to which the grantee is entitled (the full panoply of shield, helmet, mantling, wreath, crest and motto, plus supporters and compartment if entitled), but the owner (ARMIGER) may choose to omit certain parts at his own discretion.

Chapter 3: The shield and what goes on it

Heraldry started with designs painted on shields and the shield remains the main focus of the heraldic achievement. You can have a shield without a crest (or any of the other bits and pieces) but not the other way around. Therefore, we will start our heraldry lesson by talking about the shield.

TYPES OF SHIELD

In the very early days of heraldry, the shield depicted in the heralds' illustrations was the type actually used in combat or tournament, a simple shape known as the "heater" shape from its resemblance to a pressing-iron. As heraldry became more of an art form, all sorts of odd shapes were devised, many of them having little in common with real shields. In recent times, thankfully, most of these have been abandoned and the simple shape is back in general use. The shape of the shield, however, is left strictly to the artist and has no symbolic or other significance.

Shield shapes (after Fox-Davies)

"Heater" shield

XVth century shield

Renaissance shield

Lance-rest shield

TINCTURES—THE COLOURS OF HERALDRY

The early heraldic shield-makers had two main colour constraints: first, they had to use the paints that were available at the time, mostly simple, vivid colours; second, they needed to provide as much contrast as possible between the background of the shield and the devices painted on it. They came up with the following TINCTURES, each listed below with the Norman-French name associated with it:

Five "Colours"

Red — GULES
Blue — AZURE
Green — VERT (pronounced "Virt")
Black — SABLE
Purple — PURPURE

Two "Metals"

Silver — ARGENT[1]
Gold — OR

As time went on, a few other colours were added to the heraldic palette, but the ones listed above are still far and away the commonest. The most generally-observed rule of heraldry (based on the need for contrast) is that A COLOUR MUST GO ON A METAL AND A METAL ON A COLOUR, not metal-on-metal or colour-on-colour. An exception to the rule is permitted where a device is shown in its natural colours (PROPER), although common-sense would suggest not painting a "proper" white swan on a white field!

THE FURS

The great popularity of heraldry required later heraldic designers to come up with the FURS as alternatives to the tinctures. There are two traditional ones: ERMINE, representing the white fur and black tails of the animal; and VAIR, representing squirrel-skins with back- and belly-furs placed alternately—normally shown as blue and white. Each of the furs has a number of colour variations, each with its own name, but the two originals are by far the commonest in use.

---

1 Because at the time there was no satisfactory silver paint, ARGENT was (and generally still is) represented as white. The metal OR is usually shown as real gold-leaf or as yellow.

THE COLOURS

Gules   Azure   Vert   Sable   Purpure

THE METALS

THE FURS

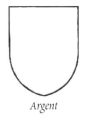

Argent   Or   Ermine   Vair

A damsel proper

GEOMETRICAL DESIGNS—THE ORDINARIES

Early heraldry developed a number of simple geometric designs which came to be known as the ORDINARIES. The main ones are as follows: the FESS, the CHIEF, the PALE, the BEND, the BEND SINISTER[2], the CHEVRON, the SALTIRE, the PILE, the PALL and the CROSS.

Most of the Ordinaries have narrow versions or DIMINUTIVES such as the BAR, the PALLET, the BENDLET, and the CHEVRONEL, while the Cross (the symbol of the crusades) has at least a hundred varieties, such as the CROSS CROSSLET and the CALVARY CROSS. In addition to the Ordinaries, there are a number of other geometrical designs known as SUB-ORDINARIES, some of which are illustrated below.

ORDINARIES

| Fess | Chief | Pale | Bend | Bend sinister | Chevron |

| Saltire | Pile | Pall | Cross | Cross crosslet | Calvary cross |

DIMINUTIVES

| Bars | Pallets | Bendlets | Chevronels |

SUB-ORDINARIES

| Bordure | Inescutcheon | Lozenge | Canton | Gyron | Fret |

2 So-called because the upper part originates in the SINISTER (left) side of the shield. In describing arms, left (SINISTER) and right (DEXTER) *are considered from the point of view of the bearer of the shield, not that of the observer.*

LINES OF PARTITION

As it became necessary to distinguish similar designs within a single family, artists developed what are called LINES OF PARTITION to replace the simple outlines of the various geometrical devices. A number of these are illustrated below, using the pale as an example. Such lines could be used to distinguish the arms of various branches of a family without altering the basic design of the shield.

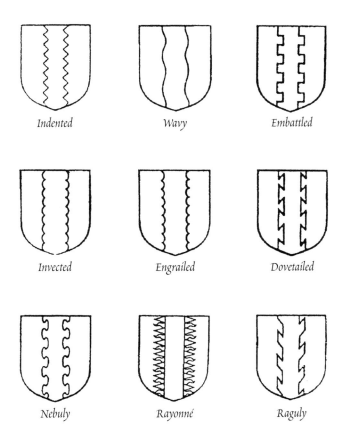

Indented	*Wavy*	*Embattled*
Invected	*Engrailed*	*Dovetailed*
Nebuly	*Rayonné*	*Raguly*

PARTED SHIELDS

Sometimes a shield will be shown as divided into roughly equal parts, each of a different tincture. Such a shield is known as PARTED or PARTY. If the line separating the two sections goes the same way as a Pale, the FIELD or background is said to be PARTY PER PALE (often shortened to PER PALE) of such and such colours and the same applies to lines following the general shapes of the other Ordinaries. (The only exception is that a field parted per cross is known as QUARTERLY). The lines of partition may also apply to parted shields, so that we may have "per bend *wavy*, Argent and Sable", or "per chevron *indented*, Gules and Vert". Note that the colour-on-metal rule does not apply to parted fields, since neither part of the field is *on* the other. Obviously, too, the rule cannot apply to devices that *overlie* the two sections of a parted field, but here again, common sense should rule; one would avoid placing a white bull overlying a black and white parted field, since one half of your bull would virtually disappear against the white part of the field. A common way to avoid this sort of problem with parted fields is to have the charge in the same two tinctures as the field, but reversed, so that colour A overlies B and B overlies A. The charge here is said to be COUNTERCHANGED.

Per pale *Per fess* *Per bend wavy*

Per chevron indented *Unhappy mono-chrome bull* *Happy counter-changed bull*

Chapter 4: Other Devices

Almost anything—animal, vegetable, or mineral—can be used as a device on a coat of arms. Since heraldry is a traditional art-form, however, it tends to prefer traditional, timeless devices with well-recognized symbolism. We will deal here with a few of these and with how they are described or BLAZONED.

ANIMALS—THE HERALDIC ZOO

The LION was one of the first charges used in heraldry—symbolizing as it does strength and courage—and we can use it as an example. Many heraldic animals are shown, not as they are in nature, but in a stylized, usually super-fierce, form, intended to freak out opponents. The lion is a good example of this. Other animals like the HORSE and DEER are usually shown more or less naturally. All animals are depicted as facing the dexter side of the shield unless stated otherwise and may be shown in a number of "heraldic" positions. In describing an animal, the position of the body is noted first, then that of the head. The common body positions are RAMPANT or ramping (a position unknown to any self-respecting animal, but *very* heraldic!); PASSANT or walking; STATANT or standing; and SEJANT or sitting. If the head is facing the same way as the body, its position is not mentioned. The two other common head positions are GUARDANT, or looking towards the viewer, and REGUARDANT, or looking backwards. So, in blazoning a lion, you could have a *"lion rampant"*, a *"lion passant guardant"* or a *"lion statant reguardant"*. Sometimes the nature or position of the tail is mentioned as a last item, if there is something unusual about it such as a double tail (DOUBLE-QUEUED) or a forked tail (QUEUE

A lion rampant

A lion passant guardant

A lion statant reguardant

A lion sejant, queue fourchée

FOURCHÉE)—see previous page. Not all animals assume all the heraldic positions and some have special terms applied to them, but the above are the common ones. Other frequently encountered animals are the horse, the dog, the stag, the boar, the wolf and the bear, but *any* animal can qualify, even a mouse.

BIRDS—THE HERALDIC AVIARY

As with their four-legged counterparts, *any* bird can appear in a coat of arms, but the most traditional are the EAGLE, the HAWK, the PELICAN and the MARTLET (a type of swallow). We will use the eagle as our example. In blazoning, the bird's general position is mentioned first. The common ones are: CLOSE (standing with wings folded); RISING (facing dexter, wings open); VOLANT (flying); and DISPLAYED. The latter (by far the commonest position for the eagle, but not as common for other birds) shows the bird's body to the front, head turned to the dexter and wings spread out on either side. After the body, the position of the wings is mentioned, such as ELEVATED (tips upwards), INVERTED (tips downwards) or ADDORSED (back to back). A couple of avian peculiarities: the MARTLET is shown as a swallow with no feet, only feathery tufts where the feet should be. The PELICAN (which doesn't look anything like the real thing) is traditionally shown pecking at her own breast to feed her young with drops of blood (VULNING). If shown doing this while on the nest with her young, she is said to be IN HER PIETY.

| *An eagle close* | *An eagle rising* | *An eagle volant* |

| *An eagle displayed* | *A martlet* | *A pelican in her piety* |

MONSTERS—THE HERALDIC MUTANTS

When they ran out of real animals, the mediaeval heralds had a great time with mythical ones, which we now call MONSTERS. Some of these were supposed to be hybrids between *real* creatures, like the GRIFFIN (lion's body; eagle's head, claws and wings) and the SEA-HORSE (horse's head and neck, fish's tail), while some were pure inventions, such as the UNICORN and the DRAGON. In general, monsters are blazoned similarly to other beasts, but a few had special terms applied to them; a griffin, for example, is never described as rampant but as SEGREANT, goodness knows why.

A griffin segreant	*A seahorse sejant*	*A unicorn rampant*	*A dragon passant*

FLOWERS—THE HERALDIC GARDEN

In most cases, flowers are shown naturalistically and described accordingly. Two of the most common, however, have stylized features and terminology. The rose, perhaps the commonest heraldic flower, is generally shown conventionally with five petals, five intervening sepals (BARBS) and a cluster of SEEDS (actually stamens) in the centre. It may also be shown with a short stem (SLIPPED) and one or two leaves (LEAVED). Unless the rose is described as "proper", the tincture of each of these parts should be mentioned. The TUDOR ROSE is depicted as a red rose (for Lancaster) on which is superimposed a white rose (for York). The lily, while it *may* be shown as the natural flower, is more characteristically depicted as the stylized FLEUR-DE-LIS. This was the emblem of the French royal regime and is not infrequently used in Quebec arms.

A rose barbed and seeded proper	*A rose slipped and leaved*	*A Tudor rose*	*A fleur-de-lis*

TREES—THE HERALDIC FOREST

The TREE is a common device and may be represented just as a generic "tree" or as a specific type. In the latter case it is often shown bearing fruit such as acorns or pine-cones that identify its type. Such a tree is said to be FRUCTED of the fruit in question (e.g. "an oak tree fructed of acorns"). In these cases the fruit (and the leaves if recognizable) are usually drawn much bigger than they would be in reality. The trunk of the tree may be shown cut off square (COUPED) or torn out by the roots (ERADICATED). (The former term may also be used to describe parts of animals or humans that are separated sharply from the body, such as "a man's hand couped at the wrist". Where the parts are apparently ripped apart, the term used is ERASED).

A pine tree couped

*An oak tree fructed of acorns
and eradicated*

*A maple tree,
arising from a mount*

ARMOUR AND WEAPONS—THE HERALDIC ARMOURY

Armour and weapons are frequently seen, especially—as one would expect—in mediaeval arms. In general, they do not pose any problems of description, but there are a few special terms that apply. An arm encased in armour is said to be VAMBRACED. If the hand is also armoured, it is said to be GAUNTLETED. Arms bent at the elbow or legs bent at the knee are described as EMBOWED. Limbs, along with swords, spears and other long weapons need to have their *direction* indicated, using the suffix *-wise* along with the name of the ordinary whose line they follow, such as PALEWISE, FESSWISE or BENDWISE. If there are a number of limbs or weapons (or other objects for that matter), their arrangement on the shield is also described using the term *in* followed by the name of an ordinary—such as IN PALE, IN FESS, IN BEND and so forth. Thus it would be possible to have *three swords palewise* (pointing up and down) *in fess* (arranged in a horizontal line), or *three swords fesswise in pale*, which would be the opposite. The position of the point should also be noted (e.g. POINT UPWARDS or TO DEXTER) as well as the tincture of the HILT and/or the POMMEL.

A dexter arm vambraced and guantleted, embowed fesswise

A dexter arm vambraced and embowed palewise

Three dexter arms vambraced, embowed fesswise in pale

Three swords palewise in fess, points upwards

Three swords fesswise in pale, points to dexter

A sword palewise point upwards, hilted or

HEADS AND LIMBS—
THE HERALDIC AMPUTATION CLINIC

The human figure is quite common in heraldry, but generally is described in ordinary language. Disembodied human heads, arms and legs, however, were quite popular with our ancestors and they *do* have their own terminology, some of which is illustrated below. Heads and limbs are generally assumed to be COUPED unless stated to be ERASED. An animal's head shown full-faced with no neck is said to be CABOSHED.

A man's head in profile, coupled at the neck

Three arms embowed, conjoined at the fess point and habited

Dexter hands apaumy and aversant

A human leg erased at the thigh

A stag's head caboshed

OTHER CHARGES

We have dealt in this chapter with only a tiny fraction of the items that can be used as heraldic charges. The interested reader is referred to one of texts in the bibliography for further information.

Chapter 5: Blazonry – the language of heraldry

So far, enough odd terms have cropped up to indicate that heraldry has a weird and wonderful language all its own. This is scarcely surprising, since the whole business started at a time when the people in power—the only ones that used arms—spoke a mixture of Norman-French and mediaeval English, from which many heraldic terms are derived. This jargon may be archaic but it has one great advantage—it is extremely precise. A proper blazon will permit a heraldic artist to render accurately a coat of arms that he or she has never seen. It also *sounds* wonderful and is one of the features that make heraldry such a neat hobby.

The full art of blazonry is beyond the scope of this book, but we can at least get some of the flavour of it by demonstrating how to blazon a simple coat of arms. For this we will select the achievement of one of Canada's most distinguished naval families, the Pullens, granted originally to Rear Admiral Hugh Pullen, RCN. (See illustration overleaf).

In blazoning, the first thing to mention is the tincture of the shield's background or FIELD, in this case blue or "*Azure…*". Next comes an ordinary, if there is one, and *its* tincture. Note that, as in modern French, the adjective follows the noun, so we say "*…a bend Argent*". Next in line come the charges on the *main* part of the shield with their locations and tinctures, so "*…between in chief* (at the top) *a maple leaf and in base* (at the bottom) *a naval crown Or* (gold)*…*". Note that the word "or" describes both the maple leaf and the crown, so it is only mentioned after the last device to which it applies. After the charges on the main field come those on the ordinary—"*…three escallops* (scallop shells) *Gules.*" To put this all together, we only need to add the word *"on"* before describing the bend, to indicate that it has charges that will be noted after those on the field.

So far, then, we have— "*Azure on a bend Argent between in chief a maple leaf and in base a naval crown Or three escallops Gules.*" After the shield comes the crest, in this case that strange bird we have met before, the pelican. This would be blazoned: "*… And for a Crest; a pelican in her piety Or charged on the body with a maple leaf Gules; And for* *a Motto; NULLA PALESCERE CULPA.*" (The motto means: "To turn pale is no shame"). It should be noted that the rule that an ordinary is always the first-mentioned charge on a shield has a couple of exceptions—the chief and the bordure. These ordinaries, along with any charges on them, are always described *after* all the features of the main part of the shield.

PULLEN

Azure on a bend Argent between in chief a maple leaf and
in base a naval crown Or three escallops Gules: And for a Crest:
a pelican in her piety Or charged on the body with a maple leaf
Gules; And for a Motto; NULLA PALESCERE CULPA.

Chapter 6: The Canadian Heraldic Authority

Before 1988, a Canadian wishing a legal grant of arms had to apply to Britain: either to the College of Arms in London or, if of Scottish descent, to the Court of the Lord Lyon in Edinburgh. On June 4, 1988, however, Her Majesty authorized the Governor General of Canada to exercise, in Canada, one of her Royal prerogatives, the right to grant arms. The Governor General exercises this right through a part of the Government House Chancellery known as the Canadian Heraldic Authority. This body is entitled to grant arms to Canadians in the name of the Sovereign of Canada and consists of a Herald Chancellor, a Deputy Herald Chancellor, a Chief Herald of Canada and four Heralds, known as St. Laurent, Athabaska, Fraser and Saguenay.

If you want your own arms, you should start by sending a "petition" to the Chief Herald at Government House. This is simply a letter requesting a grant of arms, and should provide an outline of your personal background, noting especially any service you may have rendered to your country, province or community. This is essential to ensure your eligibility for a grant, which is a part of the national honours system. The Chief Herald then seeks a warrant from the Herald Chancellor or his/her deputy to grant the arms.

A Chief Herald statant guardant receiving a petition

A herald sejant deliberant

Once the warrant is approved, the case is turned over to one of the heralds to supervise the rest of the process. Frequently, this involves referral to a HERALDIC CONSULTANT in your area. This worthy is a non-governmental person who is knowledgeable about heraldry and who lives close enough for the two of you to get together over a cup of coffee and discuss the actual design of the arms. The consultant's job is to find out what it is *you* want and help you to express it in an appropriate manner, heraldically speaking. He also serves as your go-between with the appointed Herald.

Heraldic consultation

Calligrapher

Heraldic artist

A grant of arms (letters patent)

A PERSONAL GRANT OF ARMS

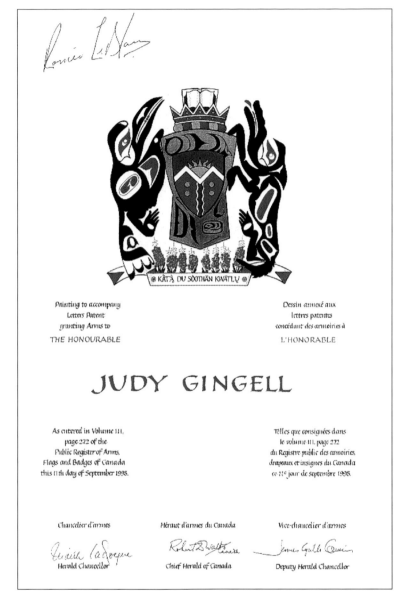

Painting to accompany
Letters Patent
granting Arms to
THE HONOURABLE

Dessin annexé aux
lettres patentes
concédant des armoiries à
L'HONORABLE

JUDY GINGELL

As entered in Volume 111,
page 272 of the
Public Register of Arms,
Flags and Badges of Canada
this 11th day of September 1998.

Telles que consignées dans
le volume 111, page 272
du Registre public des armoiries,
drapeaux et insignes du Canada
ce 11e jour de septembre 1998.

Chancelier d'armes

Herald Chancellor

Héraut d'armes du Canada

Chief Herald of Canada

Vice-chancelier d'armes

Deputy Herald Chancellor

The arms of the Honourable Judy Gingell, Commissioner of Yukon Territory
This is an excellent example of the use of aboriginal symbols in Canadian heraldry.
The shield is placed in front of a "Tlingit copper", a traditional form on which native heraldic symbols
are recorded. The supporters are, dexter, a crow, and sinister, a wolf, both depicted in traditional
stylized form. The compartment is decorated with fireweed, that most Canadian of wildflowers.

A CORPORATE GRANT OF ARMS

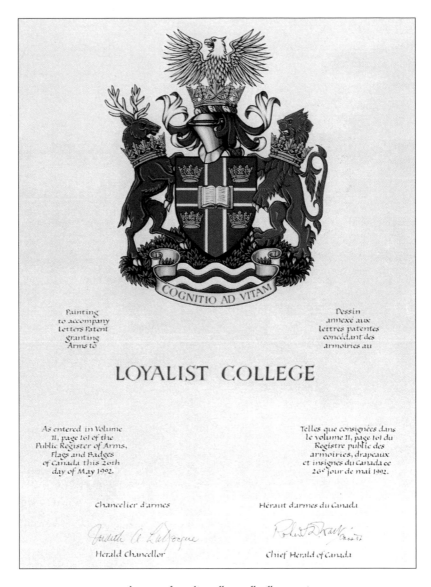

Painting
to accompany
Letters Patent
granting
Arms to

Dessin
annexé aux
lettres patentes
concédant des
armoiries au

LOYALIST COLLEGE

As entered in Volume
11, page 161 of the
Public Register of Arms,
Flags and Badges
of Canada this 26th
day of May 1992.

Telles que consignées dans
le volume 11, page 161 du
Registre public des
armoiries, drapeaux
et insignes du Canada ce
26e jour de mai 1992.

Chancelier d'armes

Héraut d'armes du Canada

Herald Chancellor

Chief Herald of Canada

The arms of Loyalist College, Belleville, Ontario
These beautifully simple arms illustrate the use of the United Empire Loyalist
civil coronet (see Chapter 11), which alludes to the name as well as to the fact
that the college is in "loyalist country".

Chapter 7: Corporate arms

S o far, we have talked mainly about PERSONAL ARMS—those of an individual—since they were the first to be used. Now we will move on to CORPORATE ARMS—those of an institution. The first user of this type of heraldry was the church, since it was the most highly organized body in the Middle Ages. The diocese or see of a bishop and the abbey or monastery of an abbot usually owned property in its own right. This property could be sold or rented by the institution, which therefore needed its own seal—and arms to make it distinctive. (See *Ecclesiastical Arms*, Chapter 8.)

The next users of corporate arms were likely the guilds, those powerful mediaeval associations of merchants and craftsmen. While we do not have guilds in Canada, the use of corporate arms by professional associations and governing bodies continues the tradition. From these early beginnings, corporate heraldry has spread and flourished and today is equal in importance to personal heraldry.

Corporate arms, c. 1400

In Canada today, corporate heraldry can be divided for convenience into a number of categories:

The Royal Arms of Canada—strictly, "the arms of the Sovereign in right of Canada";

The arms of the provinces and territories;

Civic or municipal arms—those of cities, towns, villages and so forth;

Ecclesiastical arms—those of religious bodies (see next chapter);

Educational arms—those of universities, colleges and schools;

The arms of official bodies;

The arms of professional organizations;

The arms of societies and associations;

The arms of commercial companies;

Military heraldry—often in the form of BADGES rather than full coats of arms.

Most corporate bodies are entitled to supporters as part of their grant of arms. This is the feature that most often distinguishes corporate arms from the personal variety, although not all those entitled to supporters actually have (or use) them.

Probably the most interesting of these categories to the average person is civic heraldry. After all, everybody has to live in some municipality and many—indeed most—municipalities do not as yet have legitimate, properly granted arms and make do with logos or other "advertising" symbols. For a budding heraldist, persuading *your* home-town to apply for a grant of arms—and helping to design it—can be a fascinating and rewarding task.

A civic coat of arms is entitled to include what is known as a MURAL CORONET, either replacing the wreath or placed above it as a part of the crest. The circle of this coronet is formed to resemble a crenellated wall and may be decorated with other devices. As noted above, civic arms will usually also include supporters which, you will recall, stand on a piece of property called a compartment. These four elements (the mural coronet, the two supporters, the compartment) provide opportunities (and space) for symbolism over and above that of the shield and crest—which may well be needed, since a community is a much more complex organism than an individual.

Canada

Province of Alberta

Ancaster, Ontario

McGill University

Canadian Heraldic Authority

Royal College of Physicians and Surgeons of Canada

United Empire Loyalist Association of Canada

George Weston Limited

The badge of HMCS Discovery ("disc over Υ")

However, a word of warning; if you do become involved in this process, you will likely have to deal with a body called the COUNCIL COMMITTEE, which will invariably want to come up with something like that illustrated in Chapter 12 under the title "Dog's-Breakfast Arms". This sort of mishmash will try to symbolize every business, industry and pressure-group in the community and will contain all known heraldic clichés. As a result, it will resemble the unofficial arms of every other town in the country. You will have to help them select the features of your community that are *unique,* not those that are common to all other towns.

The city council coat-of-arms committee

Chapter 8: Ecclesiastical arms

These are the arms associated with religious bodies (called ECCLESIASTICAL from the Greek *ekklesia,* a church). As mentioned in the last chapter, the Church was the first institution to use corporate arms and it has continued to do so to the present day. The practice is almost universal in Europe and to a lesser extent in Canada, although it is starting to catch on in this country. The religious denominations using arms most extensively in Canada are the Anglican and the Roman Catholic, although grants have been made to some Presbyterian churches and a number of synagogues. In the case of the Roman Catholic church, the usual past practice in Canada has been to use ASSUMED ARMS (arms not granted by an official granting authority) under guidelines issued by the Holy See. With the establishment of our own readily accessible Heraldic Authority this may be changing, as more and more newly consecrated bishops are seeking grants from the Authority.

Ecclesiastical heraldry

Anglican diocese (Quebec)

Anglican cathedral
(St. George's, Kingston, Ontario)

Roman Catholic archdiocese
(Vancouver, British Columbia)

Congregation Machzikei Hadas

CORPORATE ECCLESIASTICAL ARMS

In both churches, the Diocese is typically represented by a shield (usually charged with one or more religious symbols), over which is placed a bishop's mitre instead of a crest. The only heraldic difference between the churches is that the Anglican mitre is of cloth of gold and decorated with jewels (MITRA PRETIOSA), while the Roman Catholic mitre is quite plain (MITRA SIMPLEX). A recent Anglican innovation in Canada is to use a bishop's chair or CATHEDRA as the support for the arms of a cathedral. The arms are displayed on a large shield resting against the back of the chair, with the arms of the diocese placed on a small shield at the top of the chair.

PERSONAL ECCLESIASTICAL ARMS

These are the arms of individual bishops, priests or ministers and here there is a greater difference between the churches. In the Roman Catholic tradition, personal arms have long been used to indicate the rank of the individual in the church. The shield is used in the usual way but there is no crest. In its place is what is known as an ECCLESIASTICAL HAT, resembling headgear worn by clergy in the Middle Ages. This hat comes in several colours and bears on either side cords which end in a number of tassels (varying from one to fifteen). The combination of the colour of the hat and the colour and number of tassels indicates the rank of the individual, from a simple priest to a Cardinal Archbishop. Some of the senior ranks also display a cross or CROSIER (crook-shaped pastoral staff) behind their arms.

ROMAN CATHOLIC PERSONAL ECCLESIASTICAL ARMS

Priest   *Prelate of Honour (Monsignor)*   *Bishop*

The burdens of office

In the Anglican church, personal arms indicating rank were, until recently, restricted to bishops and archbishops. Bishops and archbishops use their personal arms, but replace the crest with a mitre. If in charge of a diocese (not all bishops are), they IMPALE their arms with those of the diocese; that is, the shield is divided by a line down the middle (PER PALE), with the diocesan arms on the dexter and the bishop's personal arms on the sinister side. Bishops may also display their arms in front of a pair of crosiers. Until 1976, clergy below the rank of bishop had no indicator of rank. They just used their personal arms and crest, and may still do so. However, in 1976 a system similar to the Roman Catholic one was introduced on a voluntary basis for Anglican clergy under the rank of bishop. In the Anglican system, all the hats are black, and the tassels only go up to three, but the colour and number of the tassels, plus the colour of the cords, indicate the rank of the individual. With more and more Anglican clergy being granted arms in Canada, this system is likely to become more widely practised in this country.

PERSONAL ECCLESIASTICAL ARMS

Personal arms

Impaled with diocese

Anglican Bishop A.J. Burton of Saskatchewan

*Roman Catholic priest
(Rev. Marc Smith)*

*Anglican canon
(Canon David Bowyer)*

Chapter 9: Arms For Women

When heraldry developed in the Middle Ages, it was entirely a male preserve. Women did not fight in tournaments and had virtually no property rights, so it never occurred to anyone that they could possess arms of their own. True, a woman was permitted to *use* arms for dress and decorative purposes, but they were almost invariably the arms of some man— usually her father or husband. For the display of her own (i.e. her father's) arms, she was denied the regular shield and had to use a lozenge-shaped one, a particularly awkward shape for the heraldic artist. She was also denied the use of the helm and crest. (There *were* a few exceptions to these rules, particularly in Scottish heraldry, but they were so few as not to concern us here).

The lozenge problem

Amazingly, this situation persisted (and to a large extent still persists in England) up to the beginning of the 21st Century, a time when women can become soldiers, industrialists and even prime ministers. Fortunately, with the creation of our own heraldic authority, things have changed in Canada. A Canadian woman may be granted arms in her own right and these may be depicted on a regular (HEATER-SHAPED) shield (although she may choose to use the traditional lozenge or an oval shield). She can have both helm and crest, so that there is now no certain way to distinguish the arms of a woman from that of a man.

One area where the Canadian heraldic rules remain in a state of uncertainty, however, is in the transmission of arms by women. The British rule (and in fact most European rules) followed the age-old convention, which still retains its value, that name and arms go together. Under this convention, the child of a marriage who

ARMS FOR WOMEN

The mediaeval solution	*The eastern solution*	*The western solution*

THE CANADIAN SOLUTION

Jean M. Matheson
*An example of a woman's arms on
a standard "heater shaped" shield
and including a helmet and crest.*

The National Council of Women
*The arms of a women's organization,
illustrating the use of the oval shield.*

bore the father's surname (still the case in most Canadian families, although not required by law) could not normally inherit the mother's arms. This followed because the maternal arms were associated with the maiden surname of the mother, not the surname of the child. If the child wished to use the maternal arms, he/she might do so by adopting the applicable surname, but not otherwise.[3]

In Canada, this is all rather up in the air. Due to the changing nature of the family in our multicultural society, the Heraldic Authority has not found it possible to make a definite ruling on the name-and-arms business, treating each situation on a case-by-case basis. The problem with the lack of clear guidelines, however, is that it could cause us to lose, in Canada, the link between a name and a specific coat of arms. This could weaken one of heraldry's strongest and most appealing features and prove counterproductive in the long run.

Transmission problems

---

3 There *was* an exception to this rule, where the mother was an HERALDIC HEIRESS (i.e. had no brothers). In this case, her arms—really, her father's— could be passed to a son, quartered with her husband's. However, even then, she served only as a link between her father and her son.

The Rt. Hon. Adrienne Clarkson
Governor General of Canada
These beautiful arms illustrate a grant to a woman
with the full panoply of shield, helm, coronet, crest,
supporters and compartment.

Chapter 10: Aboriginal heraldry

When most folk think of heraldry, they think only of the heraldry brought with them by European immigrants to this country—largely English or Scottish in its traditions. However, Canada had a heraldic tradition long before the arrival of the Europeans—the "crest" system of the West Coast Indian tribes. This system, typified most strongly in the Tsimshian people but also found among such groups as the Nootka, Kwakiutl and Haida nations, is in many ways truly heraldic. It fits our definition of heraldry in that it is symbolic, systematic and hereditary. It differs only in its manner of display, which is on household objects, houses and totem poles rather than on shields.

In this system, artists interpreted the creatures of myth and nature, usually in a highly stylized fashion, as the "crests" of names carried by high-ranking persons in the community. The animals or spirits of these designs (sometimes the animal *was* a spirit) had traditional characteristics that were supposed to be typical of the family represented, in much the way that the lion, for example, typified courage and nobility in European heraldry.

Sisiutl—double-headed sea serpent (Kwakiutl artist Russell Smith)

Raven (Nootka artist Tim Paul)

Mountain goat
(Tsimshian artist Clarence Wells)

The West Coast crest system has experienced a dramatic re-birth in recent years. Partly because it is already heraldic, but also because of its striking beauty and imagery, it is likely that this truly Canadian art-form will become melded more and more with its European counterpart to produce a uniquely Canadian heraldry. However, it should be remembered that, like all genuine heraldry, the symbols of the West Coast crest system *belong* to the people who developed it—they are not public property. Before they can be used for any non-aboriginal armorial design, permission must be obtained from the owners.

A genuine Canadian monster—Mosquito (Tsimshian artist Walter Harris)

Chapter 11: Unique Canadian Heraldry

By this term we mean heraldic devices and practices that have originated in Canada and which distinguish our heraldry from its British and European forebears. This is "native" heraldry in the original sense of the word, meaning all heraldry born in Canada, whether aboriginal or otherwise.

In the last chapter we discussed the heraldic art of the West Coast aboriginal peoples, which is certainly as Canadian as you can get. However, it is a completely different *system* from the shield-based European heraldry which is the main theme of this book. Its devices may yet enrich the European tradition, but that is in the future.

In the meantime, there are already quite a number of heraldic charges that are uniquely Canadian and many more will likely follow as heraldry becomes increasingly popular in this country. Some of these devices are relatively new but a number go 'way back to very early days—examples would be the elk crest and Indian supporters of Newfoundland's arms, granted in 1637.

ORDINARIES

The so-called "honourable ordinaries" (those simple geometric designs discussed in Chapter 3) remained virtually unchanged for centuries until the design of the Canadian flag in 1964. This presented a problem for the English Kings of Arms, since the white panel in the centre (the bit with the maple leaf on it) occupied one-half of the flag's width. This panel would have to be blazoned as a PALE, the ordinary that goes vertically up the middle of a shield (or flag). The difficulty was that the traditional pale was only supposed to occupy one-third of the space. These clever folk solved the problem by creating a brand-new ordinary, the CANADIAN PALE, which occupies one-half of the space. This not only extricated them from a tricky political situation but also made life easier for heraldic artists the world over. Crafty chaps, those Brits.

The making of the Canadian pale

LINES OF PARTITION

A couple of new LINES OF PARTITION (the lines that divide geometric shapes in a shield) have been developed with a distinctive Canadian flavour. These are called ÉRABLÉ—a series of little maple-leaf shapes on each side of the line; and SAPINÉ, the same sort of thing only using little pine-trees instead of maple leaves.

CANADIAN CORONETS

A number of coronets have appeared incorporating Canadian symbols. The simplest is a circlet entirely of maple leaves (a CORONET ÉRABLÉ) while others insert between the maple leaves things like trilliums (for Ontario) or thistles (for Nova Scotia). The United Empire Loyalists do the same sort of thing, using oak leaves or crossed swords between the maple leaves for their civil and military coronets respectively.

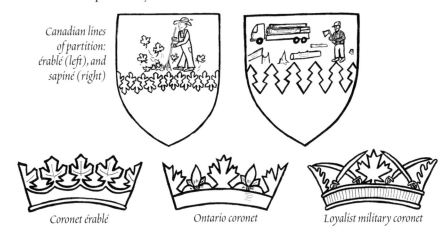

Canadian lines of partition: érablé (left), and sapiné (right)

Coronet érablé   *Ontario coronet*   *Loyalist military coronet*

ANIMALS

North American animals are the most prolific source of distinctively Canadian charges. A few are quite old, like the Newfoundland elk, mentioned above, and the beaver in a number of quite old Canadian arms—one going back to 1633. Other oldies include the moose supporter of Ontario's arms (1868), the bison in Manitoba's (1905), and the big-horn sheep in British Columbia's. More recent use of Canadian animals in Provincial or Territorial arms include the pronghorn as an Alberta supporter, the husky in the crest of Yukon Territory and a pair of narwhals in that of the Northwest Territories. The latter was the first use of the narwhal in Canadian arms, but it also appears as a supporter in the arms of our own Heraldry Society (see back cover), and in those of the Territory of Nunavut.

Obviously, there are many other animals almost begging to be used as Canadian symbols—big game such as the musk-ox, grizzly bear, polar bear, mountain goat and lynx; marine mammals like the walrus, seal, beluga and killer whale; even such smaller beasts as the otter, raccoon, marmot and squirrel; all can be brought in to enrich our native heraldry.

Big-horn sheep (British Columbia)

Husky (Yukon Territory)

Narwhals
(Northwest Territories)

Lynx (The Hon. Maurice Sauvé)

Polar bear (Lt.-Gen. J.C. Gervais)

Canadian heraldic artist—Sixteenth century

Canadian heraldic artist—Twenty-first century

BIRDS

Perhaps because many birds are migratory (and cannot thus be considered uniquely Canadian), they have not been as popular charges as animals in our heraldry. However, this may be changing. A golden eagle forms the City of Toronto's new crest and the loon (that most Canadian of birds) is in the crest of Governor General Clarkson's arms. Other birds that might be considered include: the Canada goose; the grey jay (once known as the Canada jay or whis-

CANADIAN BIRDS

Golden eagle (City of Toronto)   *Loon (The Rt. Hon. Adrienne Clarkson)*

key-jack); the blue-jay (official bird of Ontario); the snowy owl of the Arctic; even the tiny white-throated sparrow, with its repeated call of "O Canada".

ABORIGINAL SYMBOLS

Other than those of the West Coast, most aboriginal groups—Indian and Inuit—have developed traditional symbols and artifacts which, while not themselves heraldic in the strict sense, can be used for heraldic purposes with the consent of the groups involved. Many of these designs are both beautiful and symbolic—the trademarks of heraldry—and they are in a very special sense uniquely Canadian. There have already been moves in this direction by the Heraldic Authority, in grants to aboriginal groups and individuals and to the new territory of Nunavut. It is to be hoped that we will see more of these attractive devices, which are native in both senses of the word.

Moon driver—Inuit

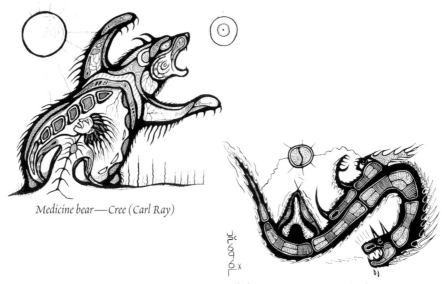

Medicine bear—Cree (Carl Ray)

Shaking tent serpent—Cree (Joshim Kagegamic)

The Territory of Nunavut

Chapter 12: Designing your own arms

S o you've sent off your petition with all the required information to the Heraldic Authority at Rideau Hall and been given the name of a consultant. Now the two of you have to come up with a design that satisfies three requirements:

(1) your own wishes and background;

(2) the laws of heraldry; and

(3) good artistic design.

How do you go about it? First, unless you have a background in heraldry, don't try to do it all by yourself. The rules are complex and the language archaic, so use your consultant to steer you through the shoals—incidentally, you pay for him anyway in your grant fee, so you might as well use him. That being said, however, you will likely want to have as much input as possible—after all, they're *your* arms; and besides, this is the fun stuff. The first thing to think of is your *ancestry* and whether any ancestor of yours was armigerous, since you might like to include some element of his achievement in your own.

Secondly, think of your *name*—the thing that most identifies you to others. It is often possible to use a very old idea called CANTING ARMS, where some part of the design either sounds like or represents your name. A good example (overleaf) would be the arms of the late Rev. H. R. Rokeby-Thomas of Kitchener, where the rooks (small European crows) in the shield suggest the name. Another would be the arms of Arthur Stairs of Halifax, where the allusion is obvious. Sometimes the connection to the name is a little less obvious, as in the arms of Daniel Cogné of Hull, Quebec, until you discover that *cogné* is an archaic French word for *axe*. The arms of Dr. Kevin Greaves of Hamilton (the author) show the canting process handled a little differently, a step removed from the name. The FETTERLOCK or handcuff in the main part of the field is the symbol of the law officer or bailiff, whose title in Scotland is *grieve*— the original spelling of the name Greaves. The snowflakes in the upper part of the shield refer more directly to his mother's maiden name of Snowdon as well as to Canada, his adopted home. Clearly many names, especially occupational ones like Smith, Fletcher, Wainwright or Hunter, or descriptive ones like Black, Lightfoot and Armstrong, lend themselves to canting arms. Moreover, a look in any good dictionary of surnames will often reveal a meaning or origin of your name that you may be quite unaware of and which may be a natural for the canting process.

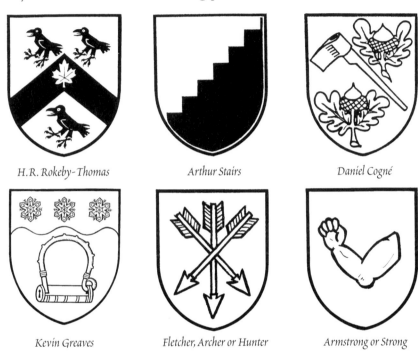

H.R. Rokeby-Thomas   Arthur Stairs   Daniel Cogné

Kevin Greaves   Fletcher, Archer or Hunter   Armstrong or Strong

Having exhausted the possibilities of your name, it may be worth looking at your *occupation or profession*. Many occupations have traditional symbols that can be used, such as the AESCULAPEAN STAFF of the physician. This, incidentally, is a *single* snake coiled around a stick, *not* the two snakes of the CADUCEUS. The latter is the symbol of the wing-footed god Mercury, who symbolizes communications or commerce. Other examples would include the scales-of-justice of the lawyer, the gear-wheel of the engineer, the open book of the teacher and many others. An imaginative example of this technique is shown in the arms of Harry Inns of Brantford, an optometrist. In his achievement, the triangular objects represent optical prisms, suggesting optometry.

Aesculapean staff (medicine)   *Caduceus* (communications)   *Scales of justice (law)*   *Harry Inns*

A fourth approach is to symbolize some element of your *ethnic or national background*. The thistle of Scotland, the cedar tree of Lebanon and the *mon* emblems of Japan are symbols that come to mind in this connection. A good example of this approach—using in this case both ethnic and occupational symbolism—occurs in the arms of Derwin Mak, a Toronto chartered accountant of Chinese ancestry. In his arms, he has used a CHINESE DRAGON (quite different from the usual heraldic version) on the bend to symbolize his cultural background, while the item in the sinister chief (known heraldically as a BEZANT SQUARE-PIERCED) represents an old Chinese coin and alludes to the accounting profession.

Dr. Helen Mussalem (Lebanese heritage)   *Derwin Mak* (Chinese heritage)   *David Tsubouchi* (Japanese heritage)

There are, of course, countless other ways in which you can create distinctive arms—and, despite what you may have thought, arms don't *have* to be symbolic, but may just be a design that pleases you. There are, however, some things that are just not appropriate to a coat of arms and are best avoided: modern objects such as cars, airplanes, computers and spacecraft; *actual* persons, buildings or monuments; words or names; any form of realistic scenery; and heraldic clichés, such as (for Canadians) maple leaves, beavers and fleurs-de-lis—after all, we *know* we're Canadian and don't need to be self-conscious about it. Remember, *symbols*, not pictures, make a better design—and it is often possible to make a single symbol do double or even triple duty.

One final word on the subject of heraldic design—above all, KEEP IT SIMPLE. Don't try to shove every ounce of possible symbolism into the thing or you risk having a design that is heraldically correct in every way but looks like a dog's breakfast. Nothing looks worse than a junky, cluttered coat of arms. KEEP IT SIMPLE.

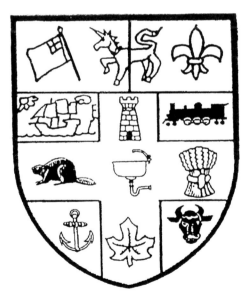

Dog's breakfast arms (otherwise known as "Arma Horribilia" or "Civic Committee Arms")

Chapter 13: The uses of heraldry

So now you've been granted your own arms; what do you do with them, apart from hanging the framed Letters Patent in the den? Well, there are a great many ways you can use your arms, such as:

letterhead stationery	blazer badges
book-plates	t-shirts
china	business cards
glassware and silverware	wall plaques
stained glass windows	rings and pendants
ski-wear	your own personal banner

and, when you die, even your own personalized armorial headstone! Your arms are there to distinguish *you*, to set you aside as an individual, to give you a unique identity in a crowded and impersonal world. Use them and enjoy them.

ARMS FOR THE FUTURE

The arms of Michael Simpson and his three children.
Note the three-pointed "label" in the arms of his son
(a label indicates the eventual heir to the UNDIFFERENCED ARMS);
and the heart and ermine-tail DIFFERENCING the arms of his two daughters.

Chapter 14: Arms for the future

When you are designing your own arms, keep in mind that they are not just for you, but also for your children and grand-children—and, in fact, your whole posterity. They will represent not only you as an individual, but your family name and those who bear it. With this in mind, it may be as well to avoid *too* much personal symbolism and retain a degree of generality in the design, especially that of the shield. Your arms will pass unchanged to your eldest (or designated) child[4], but other children will be required to DIFFERENCE them in some way, since Canada has adopted the old Scots rule, "one person, one coat." Exact laws governing the process of differencing have not yet fully evolved in Canada, but it is probable that younger sons and daughters will be permitted to retain the basic elements of the original design, but with the addition of a small charge "for difference" or perhaps a change of tincture or lines of partition. The effect could be likened to that of a pebble dropped into a still pool—an ever-widening series of ripples, with your original design spreading ever outwards, changed a little here and there by the effects of differencing, but retaining its essential character and carrying with it a little piece of your identity. That, in essence, is what heraldry is all about.

---

4 Arms can also, if you wish, be transmitted to anyone related to you who bears the same surname. This can be accomplished by requesting the Chief Herald to name that person as the DESTINATION of the arms in the LETTERS PATENT, as the granting document is known.

Bibliography

Moncreiffe and Pottinger *Simple Heraldry, Cheerfully Illustrated*

Strome Galloway *Beddoe's Canadian Heraldry*

J. P. Brooke-Little *An Heraldic Alphabet*

J. P. Brooke-Little *Boutell's Heraldry*

Stephen Friar *A Dictionary of Heraldry*

A. C. Fox-Davies *The Complete Guide to Heraldry*

Bedingfield & Gwynn-Jones *Heraldry*

Franklyn & Tanner *An Encyclopaedic Dictionary of Heraldry*

Rodney Dennys *The Heraldic Imagination*

Michel Pastereau *Heraldry—An Introduction to a Noble Tradition*

The Heraldry Society of Canada

The Heraldry Society of Canada is an organization one of whose purposes is "to promote a greater interest in heraldry among Canadians". The Society puts out two quarterly publications, *Heraldry in Canada* and *Gonfanon* which provide a wealth of heraldic information and discussion. It also provides a great opportunity for people interested in the subject to get together.

If heraldry intrigues you, you might consider membership in the Heraldry Society and in one of its local branches. To find out more about it, and especially about the reduced student rates, contact:

The Heraldry Society of Canada
P.O. Box 8128, Terminal T
Ottawa, Ontario K1G 3H9
or visit the Society's website at: http://www.hsc.ca